Madison BUMGARNER

by Matt Scheff

SportsZone

An Imprint of Abdo Publishing
abdopublishing.com

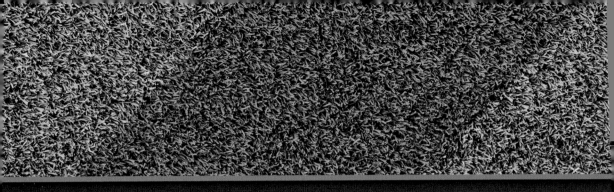

abdopublishing.com

Published by Abdo Publishing, a division of ABDO, PO Box 398166, Minneapolis, Minnesota 55439. Copyright © 2016 by Abdo Consulting Group, Inc. International copyrights reserved in all countries. No part of this book may be reproduced in any form without written permission from the publisher. SportsZone™ is a trademark and logo of Abdo Publishing.

Printed in the United States of America, North Mankato, Minnesota
082015
012016

Cover Photos: Morry Gash/AP Images, foreground; Beck Diefenbach/AP Images, background
Interior Photos: Morry Gash/AP Images, 1 (foreground); Beck Diefenbach/AP Images, 1 (background); David J. Phillip/AP Images, 4-5, 6-7; Seth Poppel/Yearbook Library, 8-9, 10-11, 12-13, 14; Larry Goren/Icon SMI 407/Newscom, 15; Chris Talley/Icon Sportswire, 16-17; Jeff Chiu/AP Images, 18, 19; Dave Martin/AP Images, 20-21; Paul Moseley/MCT/Newscom, 22-23; Tony Medina/Icon SMI AQA/Newscom, 24, 25; Kevin Dietsch/UPI/Newscom, 26-27; Jose Luis Villegas/The Sacramento Bee/AP Images, 28-29

Editor: Patrick Donnelly
Series Designer: Laura Polzin

Library of Congress Control Number: 2015945984

Cataloging-in-Publication Data
Scheff, Matt.
 Madison Bumgarner / Matt Scheff.
  p. cm. -- (Baseball's greatest stars)
Includes index.
ISBN 978-1-68078-074-1
1. Bumgarner, Madison--Juvenile literature. 2. Baseball players--United States--Biography--Juvenile literature. I. Title.
796.357092--dc23
[B]   2015945984

CONTENTS

WORLD SERIES HERO

The call went out to the bullpen at the start of the fifth inning. It was Game 7 of the 2014 World Series. The San Francisco Giants clung to a 3-2 lead over the Kansas City Royals. San Francisco manager Bruce Bochy asked for his ace, Madison Bumgarner.

Bumgarner was usually a starting pitcher. He had thrown a nine-inning shutout just three days earlier. Yet when the Giants needed him to pitch as a reliever on short rest, Bumgarner was ready.

Madison Bumgarner pitches during Game 7 of the 2014 World Series in Kansas City.

The 25-year-old left-hander blew fastballs past Kansas City hitters. His curveballs had them hacking at the dirt. The Royals could not touch him. Before long it was the bottom of the ninth. Bumgarner was still on the mound and the Giants still led 3-2.

With two outs and the tying run on third base, Bumgarner fired home. The Royals' Salvador Perez hit a high pop-up. Giants third baseman Pablo Sandoval caught it. San Francisco had won the World Series! The Giants mobbed their ace on the mound to celebrate.

FAST FACT

Bumgarner was credited with a save in Game 7. His five-inning save is the longest in World Series history.

EARLY LIFE

Madison Kyle Bumgarner was born on August 1, 1989, in Hickory, North Carolina. He grew up in nearby Hudson. He lived in a log cabin built by his father, Kevin. Madison loved sports from an early age. His first word was "ball." By age four, Madison was playing in a youth baseball league against kids as old as eight.

FAST FACT

Locals gave Hudson, North Carolina, the nickname "Bumtown" because it's home to so many people named Bumgarner. Madison once dated a girl who was also named Madison Bumgarner.

Madison began playing organized baseball at a very young age.

Madison attended South Caldwell High School. He pitched for the baseball team. The lefty's blazing fastball quickly made him a local celebrity. He could hit 98 miles per hour on the radar gun. Some big-league pitchers do not throw that fast. In 2006 as a junior, he led his team to second place in the North Carolina state tournament.

Madison was a star player at South Caldwell High School.

By 2007, major league scouts were raving about Madison. Kevin built a wall around the high school's bullpen so his son could warm up in peace. Madison did not disappoint. He led South Caldwell to the state championship. He was the team's ace. He also batted .424 with 11 home runs. In early 2007, Madison accepted a scholarship offer to play baseball at the University of North Carolina.

FAST FACT

Bumgarner is right-handed for most activities. Throwing is one of the only things he does as a lefty.

Madison also was a feared slugger in his younger days.

GIANT PROSPECT

Bumgarner never made it to college. In 2007 the San Francisco Giants selected him with the tenth pick in the Major League Baseball Draft. The next spring Bumgarner began his professional career. He reported to Georgia to play for the Augusta GreenJackets, one of the Giants' minor league teams. The 18-year-old was one of baseball's top prospects. He went 15-3 with a stellar earned-run average (ERA) of 1.46.

Madison was headed to the University of North Carolina until the Giants made him a first-round draft pick.

Madison pitches in a high school all-star game in San Diego.

FAST FACT

Bumgarner married his high school sweetheart, Ali, on February 14, 2010.

Bumgarner rose through the Giants' system. He dominated at every level. In 2009 he had a minor league record of 12-2. That September San Francisco pitcher Tim Lincecum suffered a back injury. The Giants needed a fresh arm. So they called on their rising star. At age 20, Bumgarner was headed for the big leagues.

Bumgarner shows his form for the minor league San Jose Giants in 2009.

THE BIG LEAGUES

Bumgarner took the mound for the Giants on September 8, 2009. He pitched well in his debut. But he gave up two home runs. The Giants lost the game. Bumgarner appeared in relief in three more games before the season ended. In 10 innings, he posted an ERA of 1.80.

Bumgarner went back to the minors to start the 2010 season. He went 7-1. The Giants were convinced. They called him up for good on June 26.

Bumgarner relaxes in the dugout during his first major league start.

Bumgarner delivers a pitch against the San Diego Padres in his major league debut.

Bumgarner earned his first win on July 6, 2010. He pitched eight scoreless innings against the Milwaukee Brewers. He only got better as the year continued. His great September helped the Giants reach the playoffs. Then he won his first playoff start, beating the Atlanta Braves. The Giants made it to the World Series, where they faced the Texas Rangers.

Bumgarner gathers his thoughts before throwing the first pitch of his first playoff start in 2010.

Bumgarner took the mound for Game 4 in Texas. At age 21, he was the fifth-youngest pitcher ever to start a World Series game. He started out shaky, walking the first batter he faced. Then he recovered. Soon Bumgarner was on a roll. He pitched eight scoreless innings. The Giants won the game 4-0. One night later, Bumgarner and his teammates celebrated a World Series title.

Bumgarner blows a fastball past Rangers slugger Vladimir Guerrero in the 2010 World Series.

FAST FACT
The Giants moved
from New York to
San Francisco in 1958.
But they did not win a
World Series in their
new home until 2010.

CLUTCH PERFORMER

Bumgarner struggled to begin 2011. But he bounced back late in the season to finish 13-13. In 2012 the Giants gave him a five-year contract extension worth $35 million. Bumgarner proved he was worth it. He went 16-11. The Giants again reached the World Series. Bumgarner started Game 2. This time, he pitched seven scoreless innings. The Giants won the game. They went on to sweep the Detroit Tigers. They were champions again!

Bumgarner approaches home plate after hitting his first major league home run.

FAST FACT
Bumgarner hit his first major league home run on June 12, 2012.

Bumgarner tips his cap to Giants fans while walking off the field in a 2012 game.

Bumgarner made his first All-Star Game in 2013. He had another great year in 2014. He went 18-10 and even hit four home runs. Then he had one of the greatest postseasons in baseball history. He started by pitching a shutout at Pittsburgh to win the one-game Wild Card playoff. Bumgarner made six postseason starts. He won four games. Then he earned a thrilling five-inning save in Game 7 of the World Series.

FAST FACT

Bumgarner was named the 2014 World Series Most Valuable Player (MVP). He had two wins and a save, and he allowed just one run over 21 innings pitched.

On June 28, 2015, Bumgarner recorded his 1,000th career strikeout. But he did not stop there. Bumgarner also had two hits, including a home run, in the 6-3 victory over Colorado.

Bumgarner is one of baseball's brightest young stars. Few players in history have been better in the clutch. His career World Series statistics are amazing: 4-0 with a 0.25 ERA! There is no other pitcher Giants fans would rather see on the mound for a big game.

FAST FACT

Sports Illustrated named Bumgarner its 2014 Sportsman of the Year.

TIMELINE

1989
Madison Kyle Bumgarner is born on August 1 in Hickory, North Carolina.

2007
Bumgarner leads South Caldwell High School to the North Carolina state title. The San Francisco Giants draft him tenth overall.

2008
Bumgarner goes 15-3 in his first minor league season.

2009
Bumgarner makes his major league debut at age 20.

2010
Bumgarner wins Game 4 of the World Series and helps the Giants earn the title.

2012
Bumgarner wins his second World Series with the Giants.

2013
Bumgarner is named to his first All-Star Game.

2014
Bumgarner goes 4-0 in the postseason and is named World Series MVP.

2015
Bumgarner records his 1,000th career strikeout.

GLOSSARY

ACE
A team's best starting pitcher.

BULLPEN
The area on a baseball field where relief pitchers can warm up.

CLUTCH
An important or pressure-packed situation.

DEBUT
First appearance.

EARNED-RUN AVERAGE (ERA)
The average number of earned runs that a pitcher gives up per nine innings.

PROSPECT
An athlete likely to succeed at the next level.

RADAR GUN
A tool that measures the speed of a moving object, such as a baseball.

SCHOLARSHIP
Money given to a student to pay for education expenses.

SCOUT
A person whose job is to evaluate talent.

SHUTOUT
A game in which a pitcher allows no runs.

INDEX

ABOUT THE AUTHOR

Matt Scheff is an artist and author living in Alaska. He enjoys mountain climbing, deep-sea fishing, and curling up with his two Siberian huskies to watch baseball.